Understanding Chronic Obstructive Pulmonary Disease

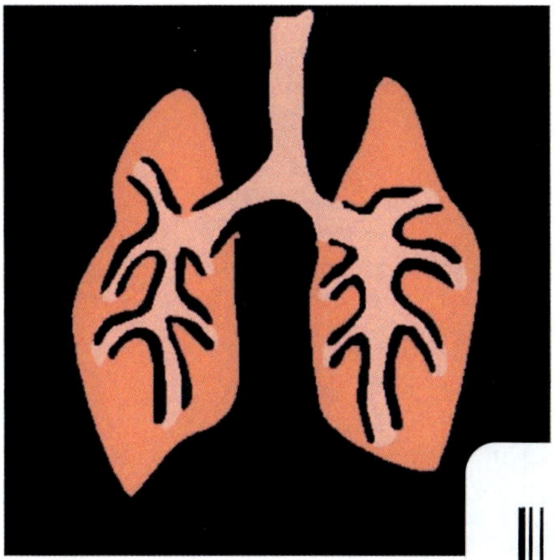

Written and Published by
Claudia Barros MSN RN CCM
7821 North 173rd Avenue
Waddell AZ 85355

Lung Basics

The main function of the lungs is to process the exchange of gases through respiration (breathing). In respiration, oxygen from incoming air enters the blood, while carbon dioxide, a waste gas from metabolism in the body's cells, leaves the blood. The process of gas exchange occurs in the alveoli, millions of tiny air sacs in the lungs.

When air is inhaled through the nose and mouth, it is pulled through the trachea (windpipe).

From the trachea, the air moves through two large passageways, called the bronchi.

A complex system of much smaller tubes or bronchioles branch out to carry air into the alveoli of the lungs.

The alveoli have very thin walls that are full of blood vessels. It is here that the exchange of oxygen and carbon dioxide occurs.

Perspective - If the area of the lungs where the exchange of oxygen and carbon dioxide occurs (the alveoli) were open flat, the lungs would cover the entire surface area of a tennis court.

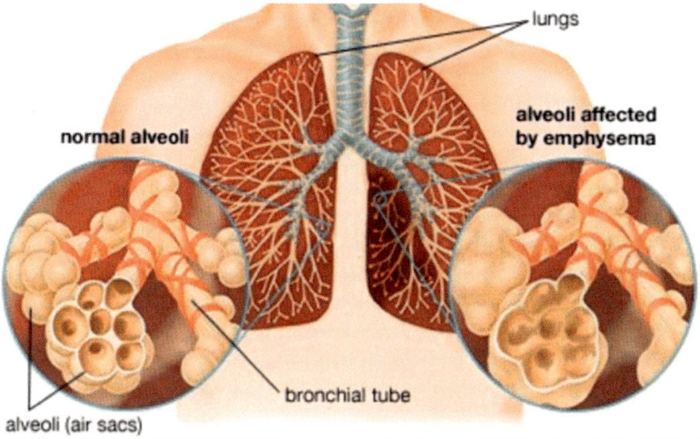

Normal Alveoli

Emphysema

What is COPD?

Chronic obstructive pulmonary disease (COPD), also known as chronic obstructive airway disease (COAD), is a group of diseases characterized by the pathological limitation of airflow in the airways that is not fully reversible. COPD is the umbrella term for chronic bronchitis, emphysema and a range of other lung disorders.

COPD is most often due to tobacco smoking, but can be due to other airborne irritants such as coal dust, asbestos or solvents, as well as congenital conditions such as alpha-1-antitrypsin (AAt) deficiency.

What diseases differentiate from COPD in that they are reversible?

Asthma and Acute Bronchitis.

COPD Facts

Cigarette smoking is the leading cause of COPD. Most people who have COPD smoke now or use to smoke. However, up to 10 percent of people with COPD never smoked. Long term exposure to other lung irritants - such as air pollution, chemical fumes, or dusts - also may contribute to COPD.

Chronic lower respiratory disease, primarily COPD, was the third leading cause of death in the United States during 2014. Almost 15.7 million Americans (6.4%) reported that they have been diagnosed with COPD. More than 50% of adults with low pulmonary function were not aware that they had COPD, so the actual number may be higher.

According to the World Health Organization (WHO), 260 million people suffer from moderate to severe COPD and 3 million died due to it in 2015. The WHO predicts that by 2030, it will be the 4th largest cause of mortality worldwide.

COPD is not diagnosed until it is clinically apparent. Prevalence and mortality data underestimate the socioeconomic impact of COPD. In 2010 in the USA, the economic burden of COPD was projected to be $50 billion. This $50 billion includes $30 billion in direct health care expenditures and $20 billion in indirect costs.

COPD and the Flu

Patients with COPD are at higher risk of developing complications from the flu (influenza) and pneumonia. During cold and flu (influenza) season, it is recommended that COPD patients avoid individuals exhibiting cold-like symptoms. To help prevent health complications, perform good hand washing, practice social distancing, and regularly visit the physician. Obtain a seasonal flu (influenza) vaccine annually and a pneumococcal pneumonia vaccine when recommended by the physician. Follow all physician's orders for medications, oxygen use, activity, and nutrition.

Causes of COPD

Cigarette Smoking

The primary risk factor for COPD is chronic tobacco smoking. In the United States, around 90% of cases of COPD are due to smoking. Not all smokers will develop COPD, but continuous smokers have at least a 25% chance of developing COPD.

As smoking rates in the industrialized world have continued to fall, rates of emphysema, pulmonary neoplasms (cancers), and COPD have slowly declined.

Occupational Pollutants

Some occupational pollutants, such as cadmium and silica, are contributing risk factors for COPD.

The people at highest risk of exposure to these occupational pollutants include coal, construction, metal, and cotton workers. In most cases, these pollutants when combined with cigarette smoking further increase the chance of developing COPD.

Air Pollution

Urban air pollution may be a contributing factor for COPD and impaired lung function. In developing countries, indoor air pollution usually due to biomass fuel (wood and animals waste) has been linked to COPD.

Genetics

Very rarely there may be a deficiency in an enzyme known as alpha 1-antitrypsin (AAt) which causes a form of COPD.

Other Risk Factors

Increasing age, male gender, allergies, repeated airway infections, and generalized impaired lung function are also linked to COPD.

Signs and Symptoms

The main symptoms of COPD include dyspnea (shortness of breath) lasting for months or perhaps years, possibly accompanied by wheezing and a persistent cough with sputum production (chronic bronchitis). COPD symptoms include:

- Chronic dyspnea (shortness of breath) or tachypnea (rapid breathing rate)
- Wheezes, rales and rhonchi
- Persistent cough with sputum production
- Hemoptysis (bloody sputum)
- Cyanosis (bluish discoloration)
- Barrel chest / decreased chest expansion
- Emphysema
- Cor pulmonale (right-sided heart failure)

Hemoptysis (bloody sputum) occurs when the blood vessels of the airways get damaged due to COPD.

Severe COPD can lead to cyanosis (bluish discoloration usually in the lips and fingers) caused by a lack of oxygen in the blood.

A classic sign of COPD is the physical appearance of a barrel-shaped chest which is due to the lungs having decreased ability to expand as a result of damaged alveoli (emphysema).

Emphysema is the long term, progressive damage to the lungs that is due to over inflated alveoli. The alveoli which are involved in exchange of gases (oxygen and carbon dioxide) become enlarged or destroyed.

Extreme cases of COPD can lead to cor pulmonale (right-sided heart failure) due to the extra effort required by the heart as it works to get blood flowing through the lungs. In cor pulmonale, there is an alteration in the structure and function of the right ventricle (RV) of the heart caused by a primary disorder of the respiratory system such as COPD or pulmonary hypertension.

Most patients with COPD exhibit both signs and symptoms of chronic bronchitis and emphysema.

What are Blue Bloaters?

Patients with COPD that present with shortness of breath, marked cyanosis, and a chronic cough indicative of severe chronic bronchitis.

What are Pink Puffers?

Patients with COPD that present with shortness of breath, occasional insidious dyspnea, and pursed lip breathing indicative of severe emphysema.

What diseases are patients with COPD at a higher risk of developing?

Respiratory Infections, Flu (influenza), Pneumonias, Congestive Heart Failure and Myocardial Infarction.

Pursed Lip Breathing

Pursed lip breathing is a technique for patients living with asthma or COPD that helps overcome shortness of breath.

Pursed lip breathing allows the patient to slow down their breathing and thus get more air into and out of their lungs.

Pursed lip breathing works by more effectively moving oxygen into the lungs and then more efficiently removing carbon dioxide from the lungs. This technique helps keep airways open longer, so air that is trapped in the lungs can be more thoroughly expelled.

With regular practice, pursed lip breathing can help strengthen the muscles supporting the lungs, so the lungs actually work better.

The Technique

The pursed lip breathing technique involves breathing in through the nose and then breathing out slowly through the mouth.

Step # 1
Inhale slowly through the nose for two seconds, feeling the air move into the abdomen.

Step # 2
Pursed lips breathing feels like you are blowing on hot food or a birthday cake.

Step # 3
Breathe out slowly over 4 seconds, taking twice as long to exhale as it takes breathe in.

Pathology of COPD

Acute Bronchitis

Acute bronchitis usually resolves in 7-10 days with no underlying lung disease.

Chronic Bronchitis

Chronic bronchitis is defined in clinical terms as a cough with sputum production on most days for 3 months of each year for a period of 2 consecutive years. Chronic bronchitis is characterized by hyperplasia (increased number) and hypertrophy (increased size) of the goblet cells (mucous glands) of the airways. This results in increased mucus production that contributes to airway obstruction.

To significantly improve outcomes related to chronic bronchitis, early detection and smoking cessation are key.

At the microscopic level, there is infiltration of the airway walls by neutrophils (white blood cells). This inflammation is followed by scarring and remodeling that thickens the walls. This causes narrowing of the small airways.

Further progression leads to metaplasia (abnormal change in the tissue) and fibrosis (further thickening and scarring) of the lower airways. The consequence of these changes is a limitation of airflow.

What laboratory test would indicate elevated neutrophils?

White Blood Cell Count

Emphysema

Emphysema is defined as the loss of elasticity in the alveolar walls of the lungs leading to the destruction of these walls. The alveolar destruction creates an enlarged air space at the end of each bronchiole.

As the lung damage progresses, the enlarged air spaces in the lungs reduce the surface area available in the alveoli for oxygen and carbon dioxide exchange during respiration.

Stale air containing carbon dioxide is trapped in the air spaces resulting in dyspnea (shortness of breath).

The exact mechanism for the development of emphysema is not well understood, although it is known to be linked to smoking and age.

The outcome is better for patients with less damaged lungs who stop smoking immediately. Since patients with extensive lung damage may live for many years, predicting prognosis is difficult. Death may occur from respiratory failure, pneumonia, or other complications.

Why does death occur in COPD?

Lack of oxygen.

Diagnosing COPD

The diagnosis of COPD is usually suggested by symptoms. This is a clinical diagnosis as no single test is definitive. A comprehensive history obtained from the patient is very important especially with respect to smoking and occupation. Physical examination and the functional residual capacity (FRC) pulmonary test can help reveal the true extent of COPD.

Physical Examination

No single medical sign or symptom will 100% confirm the diagnosis of COPD. One study found that the presence of "a history of smoking more than 30 pack-years, diminished breath sounds (emphysema), and peak flow less than 350 Liters / minute" has a sensitivity of 98 percent.

Other signs of COPD include tachypnea (rapid breathing rate), barrel chest / diminished chest expansion (emphysema), and scattered wheezes, rales, or rhonchi on auscultation – abnormal breath sounds (chronic bronchitis).

Additionally, COPD is suggested by clinical tests:

Chest X-ray
CAT Scan
Sputum Cultures
Arterial Blood Gas Analysis
Pulmonary (Lung) Function Tests:

- Peak flow < 350 Liters / minute
- Post-bronchodilator spirometry ratio - Forced Expiratory Volume over 1 second (FEV1) < 70% to Forced Vital Capacity (FVC) < 0.7
- Functional residual capacity (FRC)
    - For Obstructive disease (COPD), the FRC is increased
    - For Restrictive disease (Asthma), the FRC is decreased

Chest X-ray

A chest X-ray can clearly show emphysema, one of the main causes of COPD. An X-ray can also help rule out other lung problems or congestive heart failure.

CAT Scan

A CAT scan of the lungs can help detect emphysema while indicating whether the patient might benefit from surgery for COPD. CAT Scans can also be used to screen for lung cancer.

What surgeries are available for patients?

COPD Bullectomy - a procedure to remove one or more of the very large bullae or blebs (enlarged or ruptured alveoli) from the lungs.

Lung Volume Reduction Surgery (LVRS) - a procedure to help patients with severe emphysema that has affected the upper lung lobes.

Sputum Culture

A sputum culture is a test to find germs (viruses, bacteria and fungi) that cause lung infections. A sample of sputum, saliva and mucus coughed up from the lungs is added to a substance that promotes the growth of germs. If no germs grow, the culture is negative. If germs that cause lung infection grow, the culture is positive.

Arterial Blood Gas Analysis

This blood test measures how well the lungs are bringing oxygen into the blood and removing carbon dioxide from the blood. Normal arterial oxygen levels (PO2) are 80 to 100 mm Hg. Patients with COPD will experience arterial hypoxemia when PO2 is less than 80.

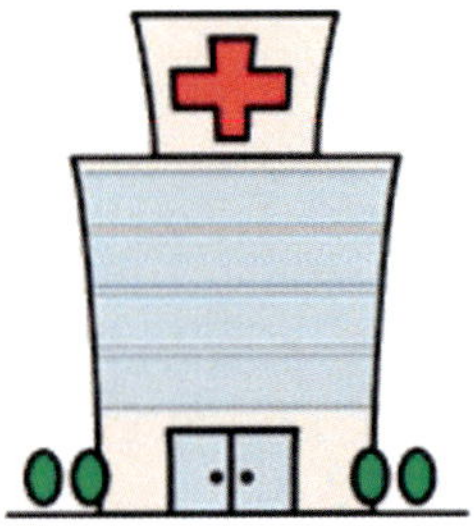

Pulmonary (Lung) Function Tests

Pulmonary (lung) function tests measure the amount of air the patient can inhale and exhale. This helps identify whether the lungs are capable of delivering sufficient oxygen to the blood.

Spirometry can help detect COPD even before the patient has symptoms of the disease. It can also be used to track the progression of disease and to monitor how well treatment and medications are working.

Spirometry is the most common lung function test. During this test, the patient will be asked to blow into a large tube connected to a small machine called a spirometer. This machine measures how much air the lungs can hold and how fast the patient can blow the air out of the lungs.

Peak flow < 350 Liters / minute indicates COPD.

Spirometry often provides a measurement of the effect of post bronchodilator administration. The severity of COPD can be identified by the spirometry measurement which is a ratio of Forced Expiratory Volume over 1 second (FEV1 < 70%) to Forced Vital Capacity (FVC < 0.7).

Other lung function tests include measurement of lung volume and diffusing capacity. Diffusing capacity evaluates the ability of the lungs to exchange oxygen and carbon dioxide.

Additionally, pulse oximetry is used to measure the amount of oxygen saturation in the blood.

What is normal oxygen saturation?

Normal oxygen saturation is greater than 95%.

The measurement of functional residual capacity (FRC) compares the volume in the lungs when the muscles of respiration are relaxed and the patient has fully exhaled to the total lung capacity (volume) when the lungs are fully expanded and the patient has inhaled. A normal value for the FRC is 3 liters.

The difference in volume for full versus empty lungs can help identify lung diseases while assessing airway passage restrictions.

- Obstructive disease (COPD) will show increased FRC because the airways do not empty normally.

- Restrictive disease (Asthma) will show decreased FRC because air movement in and out of the lungs is reduced.

Laboratory Tests

Laboratory tests are not used to diagnose COPD, but they may be used to determine the cause of symptoms or to rule out other conditions. For example, laboratory tests may be used to determine if the patient has the genetic disorder alpha-1-antitrypsin (AAt) deficiency, which has been shown to cause some specific cases of COPD. This test may be performed if the patient has a family history of COPD and develops COPD at a young age, such as under age 45.

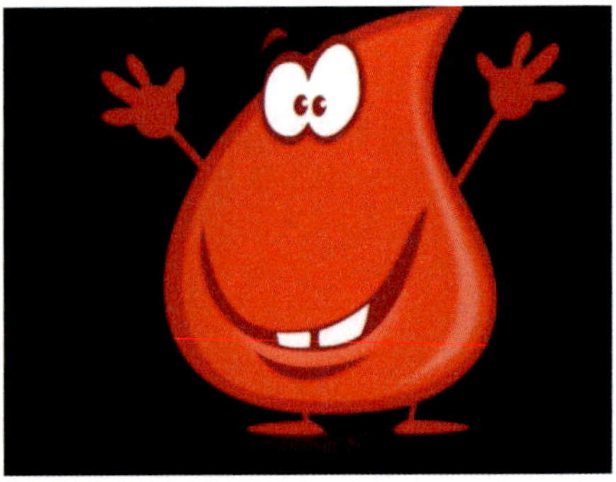

Medications for COPD

There are several types of medications used to treat COPD. They include:

- Short-acting Bronchodilators
- Long-acting Bronchodilators
- Corticosteroids
- Mucoactives
- Theophylline
- Emergency Medications
- Combination Medications

Bronchodilators

Bronchodilators help open the airways to make breathing easier by relaxing the smooth muscles of the airways. This allows for improved airflow and a significant change in the vital capacity. Vital capacity is the greatest volume of air that can be expelled from the lungs after taking the deepest possible breath.

Many patients feel less breathless after taking bronchodilators.

Short-acting Bronchodilators

The physician will prescribe a short-acting bronchodilator for use by the patient as quick relief for shortness of breath. These medications are commonly called rescue inhalers as the medication is delivered by using an inhaler or nebulizer.

Albuterol or salbutamol (Proventil, Ventolin) is the most widely used short-acting bronchodilator. It provides rapid relief and is prescribed as a front line therapy for all patients with COPD.

Short-acting bronchodilators:

- albuterol or salbutamol (Proventil, Ventolin)
- levalbuterol (Xopenex)
- ipratropium (Atrovent)

Side effects:

- Dry mouth
- Blurry vision
- Headache
- Cough
- Tremors (shaking)
- Nervousness
- Rapid heartbeat

These effects go away over time.

If the patient has an underlying heart condition, the physician should be made aware of this before a short-acting bronchodilator is prescribed.

Long-acting Bronchodilators

Long-acting bronchodilators are medications that are used to treat COPD over a longer period of time. They are usually taken once or twice daily using inhalers or nebulizers. Because these medications work gradually to help ease breathing, they do not work well as rescue medication.

Long-acting bronchodilators:

- aclidinium (Tudorza)
- arformoterol (Brovana)
- formoterol (Foradil, Perforomist)
- glycopyrrolate (Seebri Neohaler, Lonhala Magnair)
- indacaterol (Arcapta)
- olodaterol (Striverdi Respimat)
- salmeterol (Serevent)
- tiotropium (Spiriva)
- umeclidinium (Incruse Ellipta)
- revefenacin (Yupelri)

Side effects:

- Dry mouth
- Upset stomach
- Blurry vision
- Dizziness
- Tremors (shaking)
- Runny nose
- Irritated or scratchy throat
- Rapid or irregular heartbeat
- Allergic reaction (rash or swelling)

Corticosteroids

With COPD, the airways can be inflamed (swollen and irritated). Inflammation makes it harder to breathe. Corticosteroids are a type of medication that reduces inflammation in the body, making air flow easier in the lungs.

Several types of corticosteroids are available. Some are inhalable and should be used every day as directed. Other corticosteroids are taken by mouth. When COPD suddenly gets worse, intravenous (IV) corticosteroids are used.

Corticosteroids prescribed for COPD:

- fluticasone (Flovent) comes as an inhaler that the patient uses once or twice daily.
- Side effects include headache, sore throat, voice changes and allergic reaction.

- budesonide (Pulmicort) comes as a powder, liquid or inhaler.
- Side effects include colds and thrush (a fungal infection of the mouth).
- prednisolone comes in pill form, liquid form, or is administered intravenously (IV) for emergency rescue treatment.
- Side effects include muscle weakness, upset stomach and weight gain.

Corticosteroids are often combined with bronchodilators in a single inhaler.

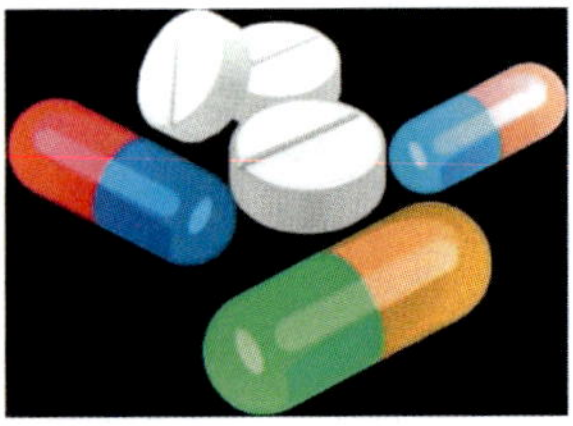

Mucoactives

COPD causes an increase in mucus production in the lungs. Mucoactive medications help reduce the production of mucus and help thin secretions so the patient can more easily cough sputum up and clear their airway. By reducing the amount and thickness of sputum, the mucoactive medication helps reduce the frequency of COPD exacerbations.

Mucoactives prescribed:

- acetylcysteine (Mucomyst)
- carbocysteine (Mucodyne)
- erdosteine (Erdotin)

Side effects:

- Nausea
- Vomiting
- Upset stomach

Theophylline

For patients with severe COPD, the typical first-line treatments (fast-acting bronchodilators and corticosteroids) often do not provide adequate relief of symptoms when used alone. When first-line treatments prove inadequate, the patient's physician may prescribe theophylline along with a bronchodilator.

Theophylline works to reduce inflammation and relax the muscles in the airways. Theophylline is taken daily in pill or liquid form.

Side effects of theophylline:

- Nausea
- Vomiting
- Tremors (shaking)
- Difficulty sleeping

Emergency Medications

When the patient experiences an acute flare up of their COPD symptoms (COPD exacerbation) more aggressive interventions and treatment will be required in a hospital setting.

Medications that may be administered during COPD exacerbation include:

- ♦ Nebulized theophylline for the emergency treatment of dyspnea (shortness of breath). Patients will require continuous monitoring as theophylline has a narrow therapeutic range.
- ♦ Intravenous (IV) antibiotics to treat any infections.
- ♦ Intravenous (IV) antihistamines and dexamethasone (a corticosteroid) to improve airway function.

Combination Medications

Several COPD medications come as combination medications. These medications are either two long-acting bronchodilators or an inhaled corticosteroid with a long-acting bronchodilator.

Combinations of two long-acting bronchodilators:

- albuterol or salbutamol / ipratropium (Combivent Respimat)
- ipratropium / fenoterol (Duovent).
- glycopyrrolate / formoterol (Bevespi Aerosphere)
- glycopyrrolate / indacaterol (Utibron Neohaler)
- tiotropium / olodaterol (Stiolto Respimat)
- umeclidinium / vilanterol (Anoro Ellipta)

Combinations of an inhaled corticosteroid with a long-acting bronchodilator:

- budesonide / formoterol (Symbicort)
- fluticasone / salmeterol (Advair)
- fluticasone / vilanterol (Breo Ellipta)
- fluticasone / umeclidinium / vilanterol (Trelegy Ellipta)

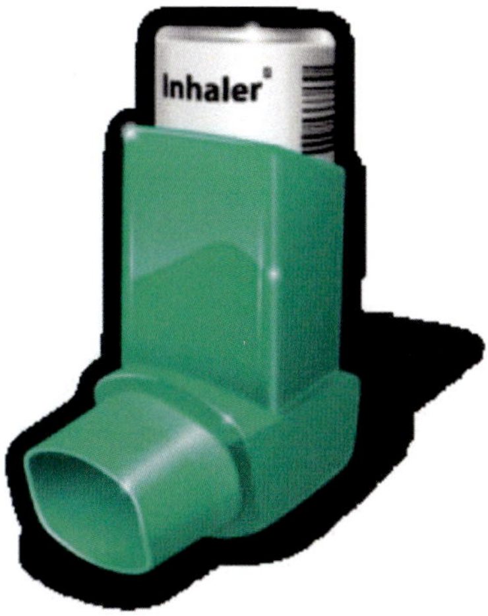

Oxygen

Long term administration of supplemental oxygen is usually reserved for patients with COPD whose Arterial Blood Gas analysis indicates:

- PO2 is less than 55 mm Hg

or

- PO2 is between 55 and 60 mm Hg and the patient has pulmonary hypertension or cor pulmonale.

In these patients, continuous home oxygen therapy sufficient to correct hypoxemia has been shown to improve survival.

Medicare Criteria for Home Oxygen Prescription

1. The treating physician examines the patient and determines that he or she has one of the conditions that might be expected to improve with oxygen therapy:

- Severe lung disease such as chronic obstructive pulmonary disease (COPD), diffuse interstitial lung disease, cystic fibrosis, bronchiectasis, or widespread pulmonary neoplasm.

- Hypoxia related symptoms or findings such as pulmonary hypertension, recurring congestive heart failure, cor pulmonale, erythrocytosis, cognitive impairment, nocturnal restlessness, or morning headache.

2. The treating physician orders the qualifying blood gas study, either an Arterial Blood Gas analysis (PO2) or a Pulse Oximetry test.

For Initial Certifications, the patient's blood gas study must meet one of the following criteria. The patient will be on room air while at rest (awake), while asleep, and during activity when tested.

- Pulse Oximetry test is at or below 88 percent

or

- Arterial Blood Gas analysis (PO2) is at or below 55 mm Hg or is between 55 to 60 mm Hg given the patient has pulmonary hypertension or cor pulmonale.

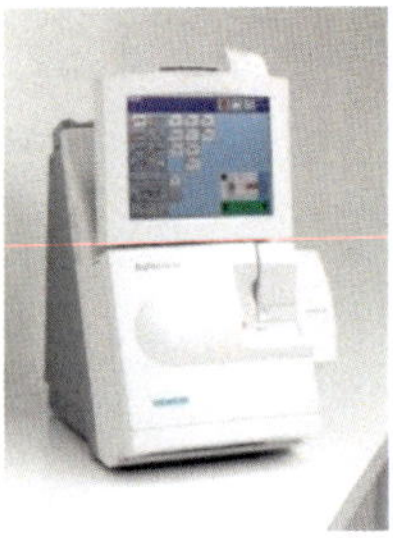

Covered Oxygen Items and Equipment for Home Use

These oxygen items and equipment for home use may be covered under the Medicare Program provided the reasonable and necessary requirements are met:

- Systems for furnishing oxygen
- Tubing and related supplies for the delivery of oxygen
- Vessels for storing oxygen
- Oxygen contents

The How-To Avoid Readmission book can be purchased separately to help patients better understand the hospital admission process and Medicare rules.

Taking Medication

Taking too much or too little medication can be dangerous to the patient's health, so follow the physician's instructions carefully.

Even if the patient starts to feel better, do not stop taking the medications or change the dosages unless instructed by the physician.

Because patients are probably taking several different kinds of medication, keeping track of all of them may be tricky.

The following are some tips that may help.

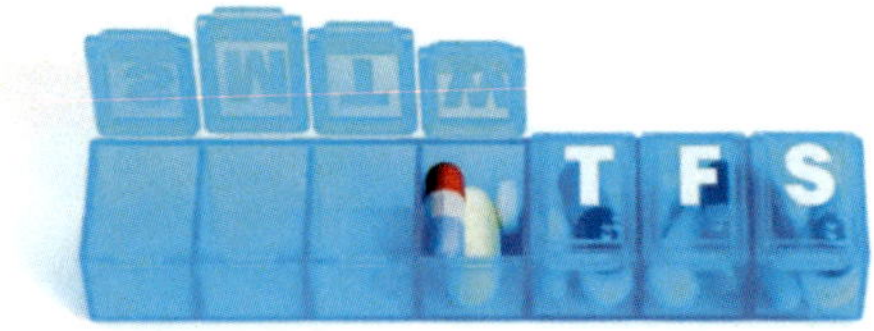

Medications Tips

- Get a pillbox that is marked with the days of the week.
- Fill the pillbox at the beginning of each week, so the patient can simply open each day's section and take the medications for that day.
- Keep inhalers readily available especially when used as rescue medication.
- Take all medications and inhalers at the same prescribed time each day.
- Have the patient schedule their medication routine when they regularly do something else, like brush their teeth or eat a meal.
- These medication tips will help patients remember to take their medications without missing doses in order to prevent exacerbation of COPD symptoms.

Keep Track of Medications

- Do not run out of medication.
- Order more medication when there is still a two week supply of pills or inhalers left.
- Carry medications and extra prescriptions when traveling.
- Have a list of all the medications the patient takes and show this list to any physician that the patient goes to for treatment.
- Also show the medication list to the pharmacist before buying or refilling any prescription or nonprescription medications.
- The pharmacist can tell the patient which medications are contraindicated and thus should not be taken together.
- Ask the pharmacist which medications should be taken with meals.

Managing COPD

Although COPD is not curable, it can be controlled in a variety of ways. Clinical practice guidelines by Global Initiative for Chronic Obstructive Lung Disease (GOLD) are available.

Smoking Cessation

Cigarette smoking is the single most preventable cause of premature death in the United States. Smokers are much more likely to develop asthma, bronchitis, pneumonia, emphysema, and COPD.

Quitting is one of the most important factors in slowing the progression of COPD. Even at the latter stages of COPD, smoking cessation can help reduce the rate of deterioration while prolonging the time before disability and death occurs.

Many studies have shown the best way to prevent the onset of COPD and to slow the progression of COPD is to quit smoking. In addition to quitting smoking, it is important to avoid places where others smoke. Secondhand smoke may contribute to further lung damage. Other types of air pollution can also irritate the lungs.

Added Benefit – By quitting smoking, patients take a huge step towards improving their overall health and longevity.

The How-To Quit Smoking book can be purchased separately to help patients quit smoking and reduce the risk of developing or worsening COPD.

Occupational Change

When COPD patients are exposed to occupational pollutants, these workers may be allowed to transfer to a significantly less contaminated area of the company. Often, however, these workers may need to make a complete occupational change.

Vaccination

Patients with COPD should be routinely vaccinated against flu (influenza), pneumococcal pneumonia and other diseases to prevent illness and the possibility of death.

Pulmonary Rehabilitation

Pulmonary rehabilitation is a program of disease management, counseling and exercise coordinated to benefit the patient. Pulmonary rehabilitation that includes Chest Physiotherapy and Coughing Guidelines has been shown to relieve difficulties in breathing while reducing fatigue.

Pulmonary rehabilitation has also been shown to improve the sense of control a patient has over their disease and their emotions.

A pulmonary rehabilitation therapist can teach and demonstrate Pursed Lip Breathing exercises for patients with COPD.

Manage Hypoxia

Use oxygen as prescribed by the physician. Notify the physician immediately if the patient's condition worsens.

Control Breathing

Talk to the physician or pulmonary rehabilitation therapist about techniques that can help improve breathing throughout the day. Also be sure to discuss breathing positions and relaxation techniques that can be used to relieve shortness of breath.

Clearing the Airways

With COPD, mucus tends to collect and thicken in the air passages. These secretions can be difficult to clear. Controlled coughing, drinking plenty of water, and using a humidifier may help.

Incentive Spirometer

The Incentive Spirometer (IS) is an inexpensive device that is used to help the patient's lungs stay healthy. Incentive spirometers are used after surgery or when a patient has pneumonia.

Deep breathing and coughing exercises help keep the patient's lungs well inflated, reduce the accumulation of trapped air, and prevent the collapse of the alveoli.

Incentive Spirometer use:

- Place mouthpiece in mouth.
- Close lips tightly around mouthpiece.
- Inhale slowly and deeply.
- Raise the plunger to the indicated level.
- Fully expand the lungs.
- Hold breath for 3 seconds.
- Fully exhale through pursed lips.

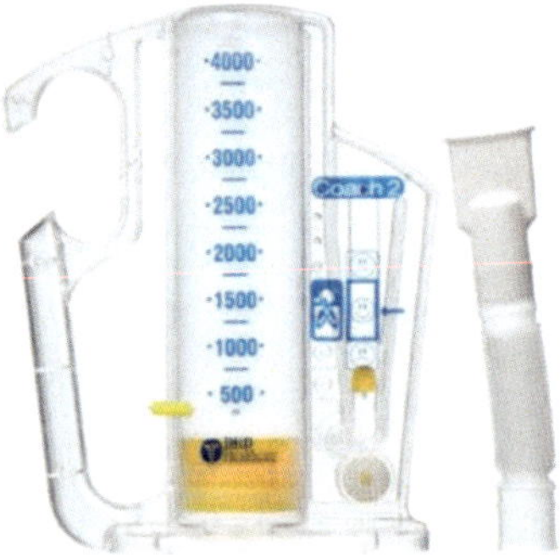

Diet

Patients with COPD should stay well hydrated to prevent thick sputum production that can lead to bronchospasm. If ambient temperature is not excessively high, 3 liters of fluid per day is recommended given the patient has no underlying health conditions such as Congestive Heart Failure or Kidney Disease.

Proper nutrition will help the COPD patient maintain a healthy weight.

A healthy diet can improve strength. Weight loss can significantly help breathing especially during times of exertion. If the patient is underweight, the physician may recommend nutritional supplements.

Nutritional guidelines from the US Department of Agriculture (USDA) such as Choose My Plate can easily be followed by patients with COPD in order to facilitate healthy eating habits.

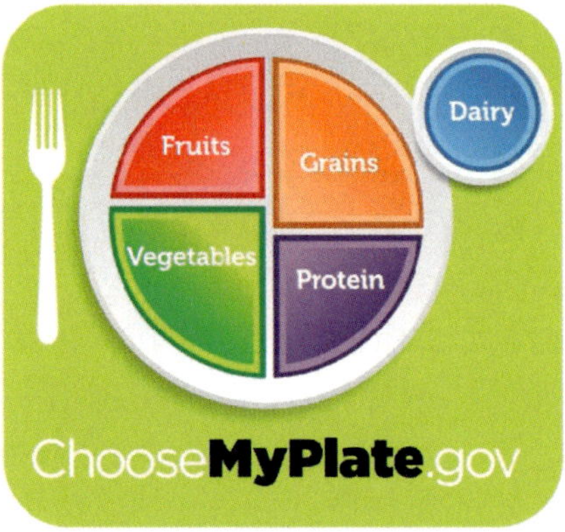

Go to www.choosemyplate.gov for more information.

Rest and Relaxation

Plan times throughout the day when the patient can rest and relax. While the patient is at rest, the lungs can also rest and recover for the next activity. Nap, read, or just enjoy some fresh air. Rest or sleep propped up with a few pillows for better oxygenation. Get plenty of sleep each night.

Exercising with COPD

It may seem difficult to exercise when patients have trouble breathing, but regular exercise can improve the patient's overall strength and endurance. Exercise also strengthens the respiratory muscles.

Regular aerobic activity such as walking (as well as jogging, swimming, and cycling) can help improve cardio-respiratory fitness by strengthening large muscle groups in the body.

Regular exercise has many benefits.

- Improves circulation and helps the body better use oxygen.
- Strengthens the heart and cardiovascular system.
- Lowers blood pressure.

- Improves COPD symptoms.
- Builds energy levels so patients can do more activities without becoming tired or short of breath.

- Helps reduce body fat and helps patients reach a healthy weight.
- Makes patients look fit and feel healthy.

- Improves sleep.
- Makes patients feel more relaxed and rested.

- Helps reduce stress, tension, anxiety, and depression.
- Boosts self-image and self-esteem.

- Increases endurance.
- Improves muscle tone and strength.
- Improves balance and joint flexibility.
- Strengthens bones.

The patient should discuss with the physician or pulmonary rehabilitation therapist which activities are appropriate.

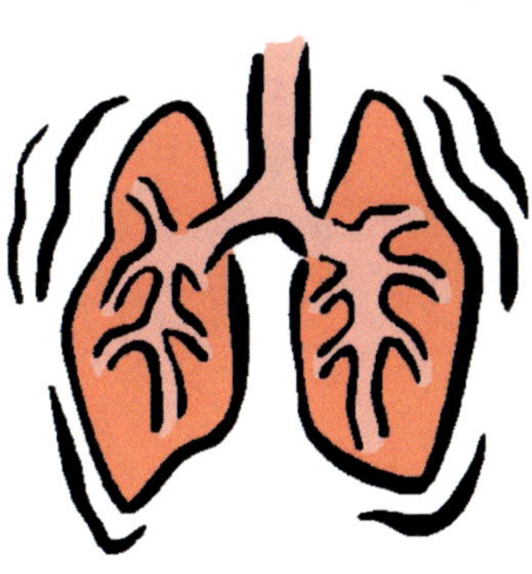

Prognosis

A good prognosis for COPD relies on early detection and prompt treatment. Most patients will experience some improvement in lung function once treatment is started. Unfortunately, signs and symptoms typically worsen overtime as COPD progresses.

Patients with an acute exacerbation of COPD can develop acute respiratory failure leading to the need for mechanical ventilation. The median survival with COPD is about 10 years if two-thirds of normal lung function has been lost by the time of diagnosis.

Even though the incidence of individuals who smoke has decreased substantially in the US, guess what groups still have the highest and lowest rates of smoking?

Highest = Respiratory Therapists and Nurses

Lowest = PhDs and MDs

COPD Complications

COPD can cause many complications, including:

Respiratory Infections

Patients with COPD are more likely to develop a cold, the flu (influenza) or pneumonia. All respiratory infections make breathing more difficult due to additional lung tissue damage. An annual flu (influenza) vaccination and a regular vaccination against pneumococcal pneumonia can help prevent some lung infections.

Heart Problems

For reasons that are not completely understood, COPD can increase the risk of heart disease, including heart attack. Quitting smoking can reduce this risk.

Lung Cancer

People with COPD have a higher risk of developing lung cancer. Quitting smoking can also help reduce this risk.

Pulmonary Hypertension

Pulmonary hypertension is high blood pressure in the arteries of the lungs that affects the right side of the heart. COPD can also cause high blood pressure in the arteries that bring blood to the lungs. The pulmonary vasculature is remodeled as the result of chronic hypoxia, inflammation, and loss of capillaries due to severe emphysema.

Depression

Difficulty breathing can keep patients from doing activities that they enjoy. Dealing with serious illness can contribute to the development of depression. Patients should talk to the physician if they experience feelings of sadness or helplessness.

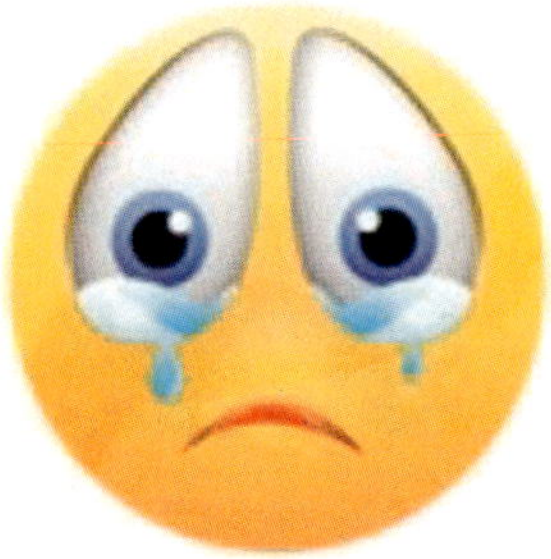

Follow-up Physician Visits

Be sure to keep all physician appointments even if COPD symptoms have improved. Bring a list of all medications. Before each appointment, write a list of questions to ask the physician.

Have a friend or family member attend the appointment. Often, two sets of ears are better than one when learning about a complicated medical problem, such as COPD.

The physician will monitor the patient's condition and, if needed, adjust medications to reduce symptoms. Different types of medications treat different aspects and symptoms of COPD. The physician will prescribe medications tailored to treating the patient's particular condition and needs.

It is important to see the physician to regularly monitor lung function, to discuss symptoms, and to evaluate the patient's risk for infection. Be sure to get an annual flu (influenza) vaccine in the fall to help prevent infections that can worsen COPD. Ask the physician when the patient will need an updated pneumococcal pneumonia vaccine.

Feel free to ask questions about the treatment plan. Take notes if this helps. The patient and friend or family member attending the appointment should do their best to understand all of the physician's instructions. Get clarification before leaving, but do not hesitate to call the office later with additional questions.

Preventing COPD from Getting Worse

Call the Physician if:

- ♦ Patient's breathing becomes more difficult. Patient feels like they have to use their chest muscles to breathe instead of their diaphragm. Rate of breathing becomes irregular.

- ♦ Patient is having difficulty talking and needs to use hand gestures to communicate. This is a late and dangerous sign of worsening breathing.

- ♦ Cough becomes worse. The cough has become more severe or occurs more often than usual. The cough may be dry or the patient may bring up yellow, green, or bloody sputum. This is a possible sign of infection.

- Cough worsens when the patient lies down. The patient must sit in a chair to sleep.
- Changes in skin or nail color. Patient sees a bluish tint around the lips or notices that the nails seem blue or purple. Patient's skin looks yellow or gray. These are signs of poor oxygen exchange in the lungs.
- Early morning headaches. Patient starts the day with a throbbing headache due to the buildup of carbon dioxide in the blood.
- Patient experiences trouble sleeping or loss of appetite.
- Swollen ankles, legs or belly. These symptoms are linked to problems with the heart or lungs.
- Fever. A high temperature can be a sign of infection that can lead to an exacerbation of COPD.

Managing Exacerbations

Even with ongoing treatment, the patient may experience times when symptoms become worse for days or weeks. This is called an acute COPD exacerbation, and it may lead to lung failure if the patient does not receive prompt treatment.

Exacerbations may be caused by a respiratory infection (flu / influenza or pneumonia), air pollution, allergens, or other triggers of inflammation. Whatever the cause, it is important to seek prompt medical attention if the patient notices a sustained increase in coughing, a change in their sputum production, or if the patient is having a harder time breathing.

When exacerbations occur, the patient may need additional medications (such as antibiotics, corticosteroids, and antihistamines), supplemental oxygen, or treatment in the hospital.

While in the hospital with COPD exacerbation, the patient may require intubation and mechanical ventilation.

Intubation involves inserting an endotracheal tube (breathing tube) into the patient's lungs and placing the patient on a mechanical ventilator (breathing machine). Patients will require mechanical ventilation because they can no longer inhale sufficient quantities of air to properly exchange oxygen and carbon dioxide at the alveolar level.

Once symptoms improve, the physician will discuss measures to prevent future COPD exacerbations, such as quitting smoking, getting an annual flu (influenza) vaccine, avoiding air pollution whenever possible, and taking medications such as inhaled corticosteroids, bronchodilators and mucoactives regularly.

Dealing with Depression and Anxiety

Living with COPD can be an emotional challenge especially as it becomes harder for the patient to catch their breath. Patients may have to give up some activities they previously enjoyed. Family and friends may have difficulty adjusting to some of the changes in the patient's lifestyle.

It can help to share fears and feelings with family, friends and the physician. Patients may also want to consider joining a support group for people with COPD. Patients may benefit from counseling or medications if they feel depressed or overwhelmed.

Depression and anxiety are common in patients with COPD. Feeling unwell, being unable to do some of the things the patient once enjoyed, and facing uncertainty about the future can all contribute to feelings of sadness and hopelessness.

If the patient is unhappy for an extended period of time, they may be depressed. Look out for these signs of depression, and if the patient or family notices any, contact the physician:

- Frequent crying episodes
- Feelings of hopelessness or worthlessness
- Poor appetite or increased appetite
- Sleeping too much or too little
- Increased agitation and restlessness
- Loss of interest in life
- Expressing thoughts of dying or suicide

Depression is a serious problem that requires evaluation and treatment. The patient may be able to improve their mood by staying active and connected to the activities, friends and family they once enjoyed.

- Structure the patient's day around activities that give the patient pleasure and a sense of purpose. For example, plan to meet friends for lunch or enjoy a leisurely walk through the mall.

- Try to stay positive and upbeat, but do not foster unrealistic expectations. Instead of thinking, "I will be hiking again in no time," the patient might say, "If I keep walking every day, it will start to get much easier."

- Talk about fears and concerns. If it is difficult for the patient to talk about feelings with family or friends, consider asking the physician for a referral to a therapist, mental health professional, or support group.

Plan for the Future

Having as much information as possible will make it easier for the patient to make difficult choices.

Depending on the severity of their COPD, the patient may still have many years of active living ahead. Over time their condition could ultimately worsen.

As the disease progresses, the patient needs to talk to family and the physician about what end-of-life treatments the patient does or does not want.

Although these conversations may be painful, it is useful to remember that these are important decisions.

- The patient should discuss plans for the future with family and the physician.
- Do not hesitate to ask tough questions about what can reasonably be expected.
- Ask about prognosis whenever the patient's condition or treatment plan changes.
- Find out when the patient will need to or want to consider having a living will (advanced health care directive) and do-not-intubate (DNI) order added to their medical records.
- Consider Comfort Care Only option as the illness progresses.

Notes:

Made in the USA
San Bernardino, CA
08 May 2020

70767960R00040